D0857781

House on the Rock

The 7 Building Blocks of Christianity

Glenn Thomas Carson

Polar Star Press®

ISBN 978-0-9801966-8-9

12   24   17   72   12   27   00   00

TO LESLIE AND WILL

Will you still believe?
This is the One who came
and who still comes.
He is true.
He delivers Spirit
and he Laughs.

The person who hears me, and imitates me, has wisdom and will build the house on the rock. The rains and floods will come, but the house will not fall, because it is built on the rock.

Are you one who has the ears to hear? Then hear.

Jesus of Nazareth

FROM THE PULPIT

At a time when individualism is the order of the day, and preference is given to personal faith and practice, Glenn Thomas Carson has written a book that calls us to a higher way of living both in the Spirit and in community.

As pastors and people wonder if the Church will survive these uncertain times, Glenn challenges us to see ourselves, as people of faith, intimately connected and essential to one another.

We are essential to one another just as the seven building blocks are for building a spiritual house whose life and legacy in the world is timeless and eternal.

— *The Reverend Dr. Cynthia L. Hale*

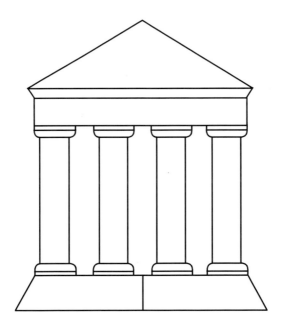

Prologue

When we think about forming a life of faith, or if we wish to develop an organization to promote a human connection with God, then we want to make sure it is built to last.

The thought of something temporary, on the one hand, and establishing a hope in God, on the other, are concepts moving in opposite directions. There is nothing inherently wrong with the temporary. Sometimes a temporary structure is exactly what is called for. But when it comes to the life of spirituality, and communion with the divine, no one is looking for a temporary situation. We want permanency, and stability, and surety. That is what this book is about.

This is my considered view on how Christianity is lived, how it is leavened, and how it lasts.

There are seven building blocks necessary to construct both personal spirituality and a place for our spirituality together to live. These blocks comprise foundation stones, and columns, and a capstone for a complete and sound building. It is required, too, that the ground the building stands on is firm and unmoving. So, the *House on the Rock* is one that stands tall, is whole and beautiful, and is built to last.

Someone might ask, 'Is it possible to build a house to last for all time without all seven blocks present?' The answer, quite simply, is no. Each building block is absolutely necessary and each is placed in the house precisely where it will support the whole. Here, we will examine all seven carefully, so that we not only understand what each means, but we also grasp why each must be included for our strong spiritual house.

There is nothing easy about the spiritual life, whether lived individually or corporately. The fainthearted will not last long on the construction site. We are confident, though, in the encouragement we receive from each other, and in the empowerment we receive from heaven.

Thus equipped, we are ready to clear the land, lay the foundation stones, and envision the completed house to come.

— *Glenn Thomas Carson*

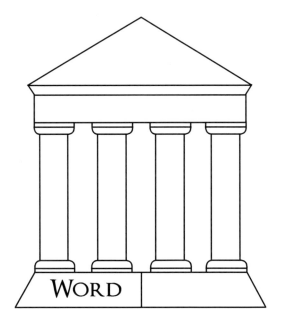

Word. It is the origin. It forms the foundation upon which everything stands. The original source for all creation, Word contains the elemental data from which all else proceeds. The first idea is at its core and from that idea all thoughts spring.

Whether we say Logos, or Reason, or Word, we are speaking of the divine spark that ignited in the mind of God, burst forth in blinding light, and exploded in an ever-expanding creative force to cause the ongoing evolution of the universe. Word, then, is not only the first cause, but remains the nucleus of everything that is. It contains, and encompasses, every thought, every emotion, and every idea. Permeating the sea of being, Word undulates at the base of all creation, rolling outward and inward in waves of material and spiritual energy.

In his "Metaphysics," Aristotle affirms the difference between what can be considered source and that which follows:

So that is *most true* which causes everything depending on it to be true. Hence the principles of eternal things must always be most true, since they are not only sometimes true nor is anything else the cause of their being, but they are the causes of the being of other things.

The first causes all the other. In other words, everything that comes after is dependent on the cause, and not the other way around. And, so, the "most true" stands alone as the pristine model from which all the rest that is true will be fashioned. "Plainly there is a first principle," Aristotle writes. It is obvious that Logos is apart from and before all that came after. Word is that pure source, a fountain, and from it flows a divinity that is both powerful and personal; a divinity that can be sensed on every frequency of creation.

The Gospel proclaims that Word and Christ are

one. The unity of the Son and Word is an eternal condition. Before time began, Word and Christ were in harmony and the two maintained perfect pitch during the initiation of all, throughout the expansion of the universe, and while the particularities of creation found their places and purposes. It is not possible, the Gospel says, to speak of Word separate from Christ, nor is it possible to differentiate between the two. When our spirits fill with the presence of Christ, they are at one and the same time brimming with the powerful Word that triggered creation.

The Gospel also connects the divine Word with the element of Light. As Word moves in the universe, it carries the essence of Light, so that darkness is dispelled, and all that is hidden is revealed. In both the visible and invisible realms, Word brings Light and enlightenment, so that in the first instance we can *see*, and in the second we can *know*. The information packed within Word is the formula from which all that is known is calculated. All knowledge of all things is inside the nucleus of Word and our knowing within the sea of being is a direct result of the absorption by the sea of the Light emanating from Word.

Moving from ontology to epistemology, Word eventually becomes words. The primary idea is turned into ideas and words are spoken and written, heard and read, so that a dialectic communication ensues to transform a blank slate into a stone carved with dreams and images that can change the world. The words strung together make cohesive thought, and the thoughts, properly arranged, form a story. What began as Logos that transmitted Light becomes a story to convey the truth of Word itself.

It is interesting to note that Christ, the Word, incarnated as a man who spoke words. With those words he was able to tell us not just *truths*, but *Truth*. Jesus, using the common language of human beings, transferred the Truth floating in the sea to the everyday life we all share. Through his words he connected us to Word.

And so it continues. As his disciples, we share the stories of Christ's love and healing, so that a hurting world is lifted to a place where it can feel the touch of God. A place where mere words become a Light so effusive that it seeps into the depths of our being and makes us one with Christ. And as we are united with the Son, we take our place at the heart of Word – and Word takes its divine place in us. That fusion leads us to take the theoretical and make it practical. It leads us to accept a calling as preservationists, so that Word is available for all who wish to bring the immortal into contact with the ephemeral. Knowing that what is most true is primary, we rely on the source, but we do not leave it in the realm of possibility only. Instead, we draw it from the sea, allow its flow to wash through us, and serve as the distributors of Word to all those willing to receive the one who is Truth, and Light, and Life.

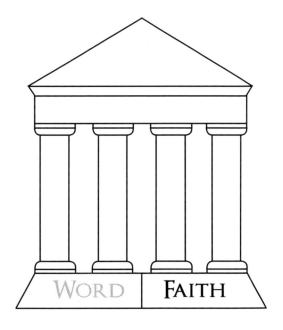

Faith. From the earliest stirrings of civilization, human beings have gained forward momentum by virtue of a powerful force. It is one that seems to be innate to our nature. Without it, there would have been no discernible progress. With it, and through it, cities have risen, assorted mathematics were imagined, and cultures were designed and evolved. It is the mysterious power of believing – Faith. And it is set firmly as a foundation stone of everything we have accomplished.

It is impossible to name a great leader from our annals who did not have an extra measure of Faith. Believing – particularly in oneself – is prerequisite to developing the kind of vision that inspires others to follow. Drawing from a deep well of confidence founded in Faith, the men and women who have climbed to positions of extraordinary leadership exude the essence of this great power. Further, they engender it in others. Who among us has not had our own Faith strengthened because of the deeply held belief of another? So, as Faith grows in one person to the proportions necessary for greatness, it eventually spills over to encourage all those around to reach higher for a new sense of what it means to truly believe.

Religion, as the basis for all societies created, has Faith as its central ingredient. To be sure, religion has taken numerous forms and functions. For most a deity (or deities) is the focus of religious expression. For some an ideology is at the heart of belief and practice. Regardless, a mountain of Faith is required to move any religion from one person's notion of reality to an established system on which a society can be built. In short, since civilization as we have known it has been fashioned from strongly held religious attachment, and religion itself begins and ends with believing, it is evident that Faith, expressed individually and corporately, is the *everything* of the world in which we live.

As with the other major religions, Christianity is grounded in believing. When Jesus of Nazareth began his itinerant ministry, with students in tow, he moved in a place and time rich with religious fervor. He was not so much drawing on a blank slate, but adding color to a picture already in progress. In other words, when he spoke of his unique take on how human beings should relate to all that is, he was speaking in a language very much understood by his hearers. Later, when the Apostle Paul took the idea of Christ and molded from it a new kind of religious practice, he was doing so within the cultural and philosophical structures that already existed. This new Faith, then, was not wholly new, but bound at the atomic level with all human believing that had come before. The Faith of Christians is different, and it is not; it is separate, and connected; it is focused inward, and outward; it is a way of believing that is both centered within itself, and spread throughout the human experience.

To say that an institution of religion, such as the Church, could not have come into being apart from Faith is to state the obvious. Believing by individuals, then groups, and then nations is the step-by-step march toward the established structure of religion. Faith is the starting point for the Church, and it is the force that continues to sustain it. One cannot imagine a living, breathing Church where no Faith can be found. For Christians, that Faith is a laser light pointed to the person of Jesus Christ. His work, his example, his sacrifice, and his very being are the whole reason that the Church was invented, and the reason it has survived the cataclysmic changes of history. Faith in this singular person informs everything that a disciple of Jesus believes, and all that the Church collectively does. Again, we see that Faith is the all-encompassing energy that drives us to search for something more – to search for *someone* who can empower us to become the people and the society that we dream we can be.

It is clear, then, that if Faith is lost, all is lost. Marriages cannot be maintained when trust (faith) is gone, and societies have crumbled because a significant number of its people have ceased believing. Keeping Faith, and sharing it with others, opens us to the free flow of divine power that can revive us and move us forward. This keeping, or preservation, of our special Faith means that those generations who follow us will be able to embrace their own believing. Yet, it will not be entirely their own, because Faith, by its very nature, is rooted in all that came before. When we take the care to preserve our way of believing, just as our ancestors did for us, then we insure that true Faith will live upon the earth far into the future and place upon the world to come the guarantee of a real connection among human beings and the greater realities of the cosmos.

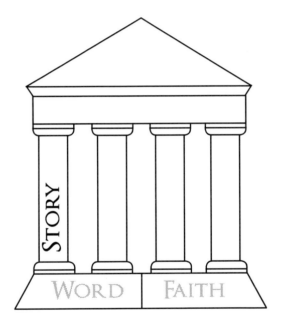

*S*tory. It is the place where everything begins. Whether one is thinking of cultures, societies, nations, or religions, the birthplace for all is Story. The facts and myths, and the legends and fables that mix together to create a compelling Story are the necessary ingredients to begin the process of germination. Once begun, the formation of Story depends upon many factors, known and unknown, to turn a so-so tale into a persuasive, passionate Story that can be used as a foundation on which to build. Great cultures can be built that can contribute tremendous things to people's lives, but the building will never stand without Story at its base.

Life, as far we know, requires water for its creation and sustenance. When space probes are sent across our solar system, the first item on the list for possible discovery is water, because scientists know that if there is no water on a given planet, then there can be no life as we understand it. As water is to biology, so Story is to cultures, societies, and religions. No culture of any lasting significance can be sustained, and in fact would not have been created in the first place, without Story. The water, and oxygen, and blood of any culture is the Story which resides at its very heart. It is not too much to say that for the health and well-being of any culture, *Story is everything*.

In our case as Christians, we were given a marvelous Story. For us it is the greatest Story of all time. The original followers of Jesus, after his death, cobbled together a nascent group of the faithful and began crafting the Story of who, exactly, this Jesus of Nazareth was. Through experience, and borrowings, and imaginings, they told, and then wrote, a Story so compelling that it literally changed the world. While the efforts of early believers cannot be discounted for the spread, and ultimate triumph, of Christianity in the western world, we must realize that not only was the Story driving them in their efforts, but the Story was the product they were delivering. The Apostle Paul, for example, told his story of conversion on the Damascus Road again and again. It was his story itself which made him a person of persuasion. In the final analysis, Story was the legacy left to us by the original Christians. It was nothing more than Story. And just as surely it was nothing less.

Human beings have always known the power of Story. From the various creation stories of the ancients, to Homer and Virgil, then Dante, down to Twain, Lucas, and Rowling, we have been formed and nurtured by Story. It is easy to see how no religion of any kind whatsoever would ever have taken hold of the human imagination without an exciting Story to draw people into the fold. Christianity became universal precisely because it told a universal Story, one that resonated in the minds and memories of people regardless of varying backgrounds. The Story of Jesus in his life, death, and resurrection captured attention, and continues to do so, because it is the grand Story of earth and life in all of their glorious cyclings, centered in a mesmerizing biography that gives us the sense that we are truly able to touch the divine.

Since Story is the *all* of culture, both religious and societal, it is clear that the preservation of Story is the most important mission there is. If a particular faith group, for example, hopes to exist in the future, the preservation of its special Story is an absolute necessity. Would Christianity have continued its life across centuries of change if its Story had not been passed from one generation to the next? One might attempt to argue that the institutions of a culture can insure its survival. But one doesn't have to look too hard to see that institutions are only shells, and one doesn't have to look too far to find fallen institutions by the wayside that no longer connected with the hearts and minds of people. The only way for the connection to happen, and to last, is through Story. It has not been the institutions of Christianity that have fed its vitality. It has been the sharing of Story by one generation, and the accepting and living of that Story by a subsequent generation, that have caused the Church of Jesus Christ to continue its lively trek across space and time. It is the Story of Jesus that brings Spirit, and life, and purpose to the Church. The 'who' of the risen Christ is presented intact in the 'what' and 'why' of his-story.

Will disciples of Jesus Christ be here in the generations to come to proclaim the good news of God's love? The only 'Yes' to that question is in the cherishing and preservation of our Story. There is no other mission in the Church that is more vital. It is, in fact, our highest calling. We have always said that we yearn to connect with first century Christians and to understand our faith in the same way they did. They knew well that Story is the genesis and fulfillment of faith. Once we understand that as clearly as they did, we will have taken a giant step toward keeping our promise to carry the gospel to the ends of the earth.

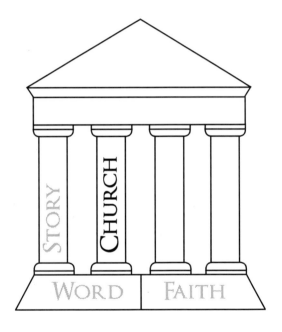

Church. The idea of a gathered body of believers has always been at the center of Christianity. From the very beginning, Jesus of Nazareth called people of faith to follow him, not just individually, but corporately. Early leaders lost no time in fortifying the sense of togetherness in the days following the death of Jesus. Second generation leaders, like the Apostle Paul, worked feverishly to plant congregations all over their world.

The faithful who found themselves in Rome in the first century *CE* were soon followed by an institution that made its way across Europe, and beyond. Reformers, denominations, and sects ultimately placed their own marks on the identity and structure of Christianity. And, for many the ideal has been that there is only one Church upon the earth.

In it all, distinctions must be made between Christ's Church in its universal, invisible form, and in its local, visible (physical) expressions. Or to put it another way: on the one hand there is *Church* and, on the other, there is *church*.

As one reads the steadfast pleadings in the 'High Priestly Prayer' of John, chapter 17, one can almost hear the rich tones of love and devotion emanating from the heart of Christ. He speaks in heavenly prose about all those who believe in him, both in the primitive settings of the first century Levant, and throughout all ages, whether near or far. Particularly fascinating are the words captured by John in the latter part of the prayer, in which Christ is characterized as beseeching the divine on behalf of those disciples who would come later (including you and me). It is here, especially, that he intones his deep wish for the unity of his followers, and that placed poignantly within the tableau of his last night on earth. In the texture of this sanctified prayer, then, is a keen focus on the Church as a whole; the Church in its universal reality.

We surmise, too, that Thomas Campbell, writing more than two hundred years ago in his 'Declaration and Address,' had more in mind than the simple physical presence of a congregation. When he writes of the essence and purpose of Christ's Church, and that Church as a united whole, he must certainly mean the universal Church before he localizes to any individual church. The ideal of oneness throughout the body of Christ presupposes that one's intent is to draw attention to the grander scale of *ecclesia*, rather than the more limited practice of *synagogue*.

Shall we trivialize the bold statements of our forebears like Campbell, not to mention the impassioned prayer of our Lord, by relinquishing our call as members of the one, universal Church? Or shall we embrace the divine vision offered by both of a Church that exists in every place throughout all eternity? For some church seems to be all there is; for others the perfect beatitude, to borrow a term from Emerson, is experienced in Church.

To be sure, the visible expressions of Christ's disciples, whether in our own era or those previously, are integral to the fulfillment of the mission we have accepted. It is in personal faithfulness, generation to generation, that the good news of a relationship with God through Christ is passed along. The scope of a visible church, in multi-layered ministries, is how spiritual comfort becomes real in a hurting world. However, we must not risk losing our intent and calling as ambassadors of the Church in its eternal excellency by projecting the belief that the local is somehow preferable to the universal. Church must be the progenitor of church, not the other way around.

We are members of an invisible, and indivisible, body that looks to Christ as its head, and all faithful persons, in heaven and in earth, of all time and eternity, as its parts. It is a body full of God's glory and one that transcends any special lodging of divine presence in scenario or locale. In the end, it will matter little whether particular expressions have been mapped and plotted. Instead, the magnificent matter will be found in the timeless abiding of the risen Christ with his one, consonant Church.

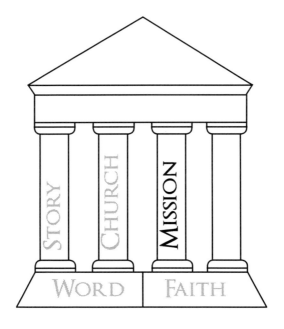

Mission. It is a word that stirs up our deepest emotions and our strongest desires. On a personal level, each of us wants to complete the specific work that we have laid out for the short-term and for a lifetime. The proverbial 'man on a mission' conjures the image of one so dedicated to a singular calling that nothing, and no one, will deter him from completing the task and reaching his goal. The Mission becomes the all-consuming focus of his life and the last drop of his energy is poured into its fulfillment.

The power of the word is compounded when we move from the personal to the general; from the individual to the corporate. As Christians we understand that the many always supercedes the one. And it is so with Mission. *Our* Mission together always takes its place at the head of the table, while *my* Mission must of necessity move to the foot. This is not to imply that the individual has less value, or that personal objectives are somehow unworthy of endeavor. It is to assert, however, that a biblical model and ethic require that a goal set by any one person must, when the Spirit directs, be suppressed in favor of a goal taken up by the whole group.

It is easy to see this distinction when one considers the Great Commission given to all disciples by the risen Christ. "Go," he commands us, "baptize and teach and encourage others to follow me" (MT 28:18-20). Christ did not, and does not, separate us into enclaves of individuals, or even of small groups, but rather speaks to all his Church, for all time, at once. The Mission he gives to us becomes the overarching *raison d'être* for all Christians everywhere. And it is our 'reason to be' in all times, regardless of items that may arise on a given calendar that momentarily capture our attention.

Since the Great Commission is stated generally, so that it applies universally, it serves as the foundation for all particular Mission, when undertaken as a solitary venture, or for a grouping of Missions, when launched in a plurality. We are unable to classify an activity as 'Christian Mission' that does not find its genesis in the command given by Christ. May worthy activities be performed that are not especially Christian in nature? Certainly. But, if we are to involve the Gospel in an enterprise, and if the Mission is to carry a sacramental label that includes the imprimatur of the risen Christ, then it is requisite that the enterprise be grounded in the Commission given to us personally by Jesus.

In this we appreciate that a careful vetting must be employed when choosing which Mission, or Missions, to initiate. And attention must continue to be given to insure that the Mission, as it unfolds, remains within its given Christian parameters, and that it remains a viable contribution to the cause for which it was begun. Simply because a specific Mission was started does not of necessity mean that it should be continued, or even completed. As circumstances evolve it is possible that what started as a creditable project no longer meets needs or goals as they currently exist. This is why such care must be given at every juncture, because a Mission should not be abandoned whimsically, or due to a change in vogue, but can be altered or cancelled when it is clear from prayerful observation that it has ceased to function in its original, or subsequent, formation.

It is also clear that it is possible, even desirable, to class individual Missions, so that the ones that have the most lasting value for the cause of Christ receive the majority of our interest and priority in our stewardship. Those examples of Mission which are more universal in nature would, then, be graded higher than those of more local character. And those which serve the cause for a longer period of time would, generally speaking, take precedence over those which appear on the scene briefly. This logical approach to choosing and continuing Mission secures those endeavors which tend to lean toward eternity, while those trapped within space-time are allowed to conclude.

From the preceding, it arises that those Missions which convey the essence of Christ's Church forward to subsequent generations would be classed among the universal, or eternal, ventures (or organizations), and those which serve only the time and place of residence would be categorized otherwise. It can be proposed, too, that the essence is defined as the biography of Jesus Christ, his teachings and life-affirming principles expressed, and the stories which have given evidence to his divine activity across the ages. Since the biography, teachings, and principles are set and unchanging, the expansion of the substantive core of Christianity turns upon the stories. It is the preservation of these stories, then, which becomes the primary Mission and highest calling of each Christian, and of the Church in totality, so that the Gospel is transported from this generation, to the next, and onto the next.

With these premises in mind, one finds that it is not too bold to assert that the ultimate Mission is safeguarding the story and dispatching its message throughout the earth, both now and in the future. That is to say, the story is the authentic Mission articulated in our world, and retained for the one to come.

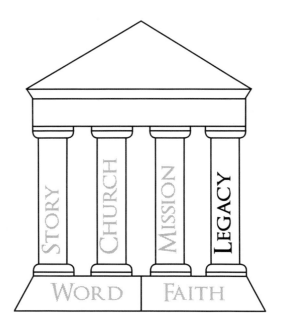

egacy. It is a word that is much used with an individual tilt. We ask, *What will your Legacy be?* That is an important question and one which each of us should seriously consider. Personal Legacy for family and for vocation forms the frame in which each one of us will be remembered. The desire to be remembered is as much a part of the human condition as the desire to procreate. And not just remembered, but remembered for some outstanding trait of character, or contribution to the greater good. A grounded, established Legacy that places *my name* among the twinkling stars of great accomplishment: each person yearns for such status.

As elemental as the desire for personal Legacy is, it pales in the light of the Christian idea of what Legacy is all about. Just as the New Testament almost always uses the address 'you' in the plural, so our Christian path to Legacy is not so much the journey of an individual, but the joint-steps that can only be taken in, and with, a community. The real question, then, is *What will our Legacy be?*

The life of faith in service to our Lord places us, automatically, as a spiritual community, in a stance of looking more outward than inward. Must my personal relationship with Christ be so healthy that I am growing in my likeness to him? Yes. But that personal relationship is only a beginning in the life of faith, not an ending.

Each person growing individually in spirit and grace strengthens each for the purpose of increasing the vitality of the whole community. The entire Church is the Body of Christ, correct? And individual believers are only parts, members of that whole, holy Body. The testimony of every book of the Bible is that God primarily reaches out to *us* and only afterwards reaches out to *me*. We speak of 'the life' (singular) of faith, not 'lives' (plural), because it is a greater life beyond ourselves that we are sharing in. It is, in fact, a life lived together at the very center of the source of life: the heart of Jesus Christ.

This knowledge heightens our sense of connection with the human family. Every person born appears on planet earth as a result of two persons joining to initiate a new life. From the very beginning, then, each one of us is intimately connected to other people. It is not too much to say that, quite literally, *we are other people*. We are born as a result of the most tender human community, and we are born, from the first day, into a community of all human beings. Our connections are so fundamental to our nature that one might consider it a contrivance to individuate and separate. "It's well known," Sir Isaac Newton writes in *Opticks*, "that Bodies act upon one another by the Attractions of Gravity, Magnetism and Electricity." Such is the "tenor and course of nature," he adds. Attraction to one another, and the fusing of all, is at the core of our makeup.

More particularly, those of us 'in Christ' belong to the community of faith that traces its connections over the course of two thousand years, tens of thousands of locales, and billions of believers. I do not stand alone, nor does a congregation, regardless of place or time, stand alone.

The Holy Spirit moves along the timeline, lives among the people, and re-creates the many into one, so that the universal, timeless Body of Christ exists in a spiritual harmony that transcends all. Far from being cut-off and alone, no matter the circumstances experienced, each believer, and each singular community, is born from the intimate relationship of the triune God, and born to the eternal bond of connectivity in the Spirit.

Understanding these truths produces a clear, unequivocal answer to our deeply held question: *What will our Legacy be?* Our Legacy will be precisely that which we were born to. It will be that which we have abided in all our days. Our Legacy together is our life together – the life of faith. And faith is an action; it is doing. Faith is working to bring about the peace of Christ among all people the world over. Faith is sharing in the communally held belief that this life we cherish is worthy of devotion. We inherited this life of Christian community, we live it connected to the joys and challenges of the whole Body, and we stand ready to pass it on to the next generation of this very same family, so that at once the life of faith is delivered and the Legacy itself remains intact, and glorious, and alive.

*S*pirit. Within the suspension of space, time, and eternity a connectivity agent works to insure the cohesion and compatibility of all that is. That sounds complicated. And it is. We live in an intricately balanced universe, where the smallest movement of one particle affects the course of millions of others. Those millions, joined to an active force, affect more millions, until the outcomes that seemed to be sure only moments before are diverted to accomplish wholly different outcomes, which may, in the end, have been the ones destined all along. In this process, which can take only micro-seconds, the Spirit lives, and moves, and performs.

The whole of the universe concentrated into one thought. Can you imagine? All that ever was, or ever will be, made a singularity of person, and power, and principle. When we encounter Spirit we come into direct contact with the unstoppable force that caused everything to ignite – and everything to continue.

When we breathe, we inhale Spirit. When we

think, we process Spirit. When we speak, we exhale Spirit. When we act, or are at rest, whether we are moving or sitting still, we do all within the essence of Spirit, and Spirit does all within us. When will we advance? When Spirit gives the word. When will we stop? As soon as Spirit says 'enough.' Our being depends entirely upon Spirit, and not the other way around.

Jesus of Nazareth was intimately connected with Spirit. One doesn't have to search very far in his biography to realize that his whole life was wrapped in a brightly colored paper with 'Spirit' written all across it. When he stopped to pray; when he reached out to heal; when he spoke the truth; when he extended his arms to embrace; when he walked away; when he responded, either in love or in anger, it was all under the canopy of Spirit, who not only filled our Lord, but directed each step he ever took. It is impossible to separate Jesus from Spirit and have either person, or idea, make sense. As Jesus acted, so the Spirit acted. As the Spirit moved from one locale to another, so Jesus followed and placed his footprints in exactly the same places. As Christians, when we say we are filled up with the Spirit, we are at one and the same time saying that Jesus so permeates our hearts and souls that we are one with him, and his life has become our life.

Whether we are speaking of our lives as individuals, or our one life together, what is certain is that Spirit flows through us with such energy that we are animated, personally and corporately, to fulfill our destiny. If that sounds too grand, then you have yet to gain at least an elementary understanding of Spirit. We are considering, here, the universal force that causes all things to be, acts within all things, and flows between all, so that unity is possible. The Apostle said that 'in Christ all things hold together.' That is it precisely. It is not just *because* of Spirit, but *in* Spirit that the interlocking of every molecule happens and makes possible the One out of the Many. Spirit makes real that which before was only an idea.

We know, too, that when all else has passed away, Spirit remains. It is the constancy that we long for and the permanency that we most desire. Just as our very breath gives witness to Spirit, so our voices join to exclaim this foundational truth: Spirit is everything; everything is Spirit. Since that is so, it follows that our life of faith receives its power from the Spirit. To say that we have faith, but we have no Spirit is nonsensical. Equally nonsensical would be to say we have the Spirit, but we have no faith. My breath and the Spirit are one. And my faith and the Spirit are one. The Spirit empowers my faith, and thus filled, I am able to do faithful things and, ultimately, carry faith back to its source in the heart of God.

It is easy to see how Spirit is the capstone of our life as Christians. All the pieces of faithful living must find their proper place, but once there, each lifts and exalts the one element that is over all, and through all, and in all: the power of Spirit.

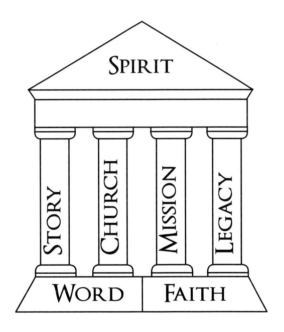

EPILOGUE

Seven building blocks. Seven ideas. One house – yes – but one that is comprised of seven elements, each absolutely necessary to make the whole. Beginning with Word and ending with Spirit, we see that the house is constructed, brick-by-brick, so that when finished it stands ready to last for all eternity, placed firmly on the hill, so that it can be seen, and approached, from wherever the seeker may find himself.

If you have read thoughtfully, you have discovered the thread of the universal. The local has its place, and it is where we find ourselves in mundanity, but when the greater desire takes hold, and we wish to move up to the higher levels of reality, then we understand that the universal awaits us with lessons in hand. These are lessons that are sublime in their essence, and stunning in their appearance. And these are the lessons we must learn if we hope to understand who we truly are, to discern reality as it actually is, and discover how *we* and *is* interact and interfuse.

The universal is the pinnacle of discernment. And, once reached, enables the individual spirit to move beyond the trappings of time, space, and place. With our hopes set in the universal, we let go of those temporary structures, and hold the eternal in hands readied with the tools to build those structures that are timeless.

In living out Christianity individually and corporately, we realize that we need a place that nurtures our energies; a place that allows us to become the faithful people that we long to be. That place is the *House on the Rock*. The building blocks have already been made. But it is up to us to put them in their proper places, to add the mortar and reinforcement, and carefully hew each stone and column. When we have built our spiritual house in the way prescribed by tradition and universal knowledge, then we can be sure that the house will serve us in our quest to fulfill God's mission, and we can be confident that it has been built to last.

While one understands the universality of all that has been said, there is also the underlying truth of what has not been said. That is, when one has delineated the whole of what is, then all of what is not moves expeditiously to the forefront, just as a blue-green prism of sunlight encounters atmosphere. In other words, the traveler reaches the shore just as the sunrise addresses the horizon, and masters the eastern light, so that the true meets the true at exactly the right moment.

~Verum est universalis~

Recommended Reading

Albert the Great, *On Union with God*

Aristotle, *Metaphysics*

Marcus Aurelius, *Meditations*

Richard Bach, *Illusions*

Boethius, *The Consolation of Philosophy*

Joseph Campbell, *Myths to Live By*

Ralph Waldo Emerson, *Spiritual Laws*

Justo L. González, *The Story of Christianity*

Archibald M. Hunter, *The Message of the New Testament*

St. John of the Cross, *Ascent of Mount Carmel*

Thomas à Kempis, *The Imitation of Christ*

Julian of Norwich, *Showings*

Alister E. McGrath, *Christian Theology*

Thomas Merton, *Thoughts in Solitude*

J. Keith Miller, *The Secret Life of the Soul*

Earl Nightingale, *The Strangest Secret*

Origen of Alexandria, *On First Principles*

M. Scott Peck, *In Heaven as on Earth*

J.B. Phillips, *New Testament Christianity*

Jim Rohn, *Leading an Inspired Life*

Edward Gordon Selwyn, ed., *A Short History of Christian Thought*

John Shelby Spong, *Resurrection: Myth or Reality?*

Paul Tillich, *A History of Christian Thought*

Leo Tolstoy, *What Men Live By*

H.G. Wells, *A Short History of the World*

Walt Whitman, *Song of Myself*

$10

Glenn Thomas Carson, A.S., B.F.A., M.Div., Ph.D. is the President and Chief Historian of Disciples of Christ Historical Society. He is the author of *The Eternity Principle* and *Finding the Right Path*.

Polar Star Press
Nashville, Tennessee

www.PolarStarPress.com

978-0-9801966-8-9

ISBN: 978-0-9801966-8-9

9 780980 196689

51000